The Old Man and the Sea
Study Guide

by Calvin Roso

Limited permission to reproduce this study guide.

Purchase of this study guide entitles an individual teacher
to reproduce pages for use in the classroom or home.
Multiple teachers may not reproduce pages
from the same study guide.

The Old Man and the Sea Study Guide
A Progeny Press Study Guide
by Calvin Roso
with Michael Gilleland, Andrew Clausen

Copyright © 2000 Progeny Press
All rights reserved.

Reproduction or translation of any part of this work
beyond that permitted by Section 107 or 108 of the
1976 United States Copyright Act without the written
permission of the copyright owner is unlawful.
Requests for permission or other information should be
addressed to Reprint Permissions, Progeny Press,
PO Box 100, Fall Creek, WI 54742-0100.

Printed in the United States of America.

ISBN: 978-1-58609-376-1 Book
        978-1-58609-249-8 CD
        978-1-58609-468-3 Set

Table of Contents

Note to Instructor

How to Use Progeny Press Study Guides.   Progeny Press study guides are designed to help students better understand and enjoy literature by getting them to notice and understand how authors craft their stories and to show them how to think through the themes and ideas introduced in the stories. To properly work through a Progeny Press study guide, students should have easy access to a good dictionary, a thesaurus, a Bible (we use NIV translation, but that is up to your preference; just be aware of some differences in language), and sometimes a topical Bible or concordance. Supervised access to the Internet also can be helpful at times, as can a good set of encyclopedias.

Most middle grades and high school study guides take from eight to ten weeks to complete, generally working on one section per week. Over the years, we have found that it works best if the students completely read the novel the first week, while also working on a prereading activity chosen by the parent or teacher. Starting the second week, most parents and teachers have found it works best to work on one study guide page per day until the chapter sections are completed. Students should be allowed to complete questions by referring to the book; many questions require some cross-reference between elements of the stories.

Most study guides contain an Overview section that can be used as a final test, or it can be completed in the same way the chapter sections were completed. If you wish to perform a final test but your particular study guide does not have an Overview section, we suggest picking a couple of questions from each section of the study guide and using them as your final test.

Most study guides also have a final section of essays and postreading activities. These may be assigned at the parents' or teachers' discretion, but we suggest that students engage in several writing or other extra activities during the study of the novel to complement their reading and strengthen their writing skills.

As for high school credits, most Christian high schools with whom we have spoken have assigned a value of one-fourth credit to each study guide, and this also seems to be acceptable to colleges assessing homeschool transcripts.

Internet References

All websites listed in this study guide were checked for appropriateness at the time of publication. However, due to the changing nature of the Internet, we cannot guarantee that the URLs listed will remain appropriate or viable. Therefore, we urge parents and teachers to take care in and exercise careful oversight of their children's use of the Internet.

Synopsis

We are hard pressed on every side, but not crushed; perplexed, but not in despair;
persecuted, but not abandoned; struck down, but not destroyed. . . .
Therefore we do not lose heart. Though outwardly we are wasting away,
yet inwardly we are being renewed day by day.
—*2 Corinthians 4:8,9,16*

After 84 days without taking a fish, Santiago is soon to catch something larger than he can ever imagine. It is his courage and perseverance of character that enables him to go out to sea in his weather-beaten boat each day.

In the midst of ridicule from younger fishermen, Santiago finds courage in his friendship with a young boy, Manolin, who has fished with Santiago since he was five years old. But because of Santiago's "bad luck," Manolin's parents will not allow the boy to fish with Santiago any more.

This short novel shows the outcome of one man's endurance in the midst of defeat, and how the friendship of a young boy gives him hope. *The Old Man and the Sea* won author Ernest Hemingway the Pulitzer Prize in 1953.

Background Information

After World War I, many Americans were disillusioned and questioned the validity of traditional ideals, literature and art forms. At this time, many American writers and artists sought ways to express and define a sense of hopelessness that seemed to contrast past beliefs and traditions.

The Lost Generation

During the post-WWI era, many Americans saw life as dysfunctional and hopeless. Seeking to find new meaning, several American writers and artists left the United States to live and work in Europe. They often met together to encourage each other in their artistic endeavors. A "lost generation" was writer Gertrude Stein's assessment of this group of expatriate Americans who were alienated from both traditional values and from their own roots in the United States. Some of the more prominent members of the expatriates were F. Scott Fitzgerald, Ezra Pound, Ernest Hemingway, T.S. Eliot, and Gertrude Stein.

Modernism

This growing sense of disjointedness and uncertainty required a new philosophy to define the pessimism of modern life. Modernism was an artistic trend that strove for new ways to communicate in a world where past traditions, values, and ideals no longer applied. Modernist writers often sought to strip away descriptions of characters and setting while avoiding direct statements of theme and resolutions. This "fragmented" style of writing theoretically enabled the reader to choose meaning for himself, while understanding that life was fragmented and without meaning.

About the Author

Often cited as the writer who did more to change the style of English prose than any other 20th Century author, Ernest Hemingway (1899–1961) is known as much for his lifestyle as he is for his literary style.

Born and raised in Oak Park, Illinois, a suburb of Chicago, Hemingway's first job was reporting for the Kansas City Star. Eager to serve in WWI, he joined the Red Cross ambulance corps and was sent to the Italian front, where he was severely wounded. Hemingway's experiences during the war and the years that followed greatly influenced him and his writing.

After WWI, Hemingway joined a group of disillusioned writers and artists in Europe. It was during this time period that he published his first book, *Three Stories and Ten Poems.* Three years later, in 1926, Hemingway published *The Sun Also Rises,* which achieved critical acclaim and earned him the reputation as spokesman for the "lost generation."

In the years to follow, Ernest Hemingway spent long periods of time in Key West, Florida, Spain, Cuba, and Africa. Known as an outspoken fisherman, hunter, bullfight enthusiast, and drinker, Hemingway's personal life also had a great influence on American writers.

Hemingway's crisp dialogue and no-nonsense journalistic style portrayed themes of a modern world filled with emptiness, failure, and defeat. Hemingway was deeply concerned with authenticity in writing. Unnecessary detail was replaced by short declarative sentences and imagery often based on personal observances and experiences.

In 1954, Hemingway's novel *The Old Man and the Sea* earned the Pulitzer Prize in literature, and Hemingway was awarded a Nobel Prize for his "mastery of the art of modern narration." Yet in spite of his fame and fortune, Ernest Hemingway's modernist views and hedonist lifestyle led him to take his life in 1961.

Old Man and the Sea Page References

The Old Man and the Sea is a short novel written as one continuous narrative. There are no chapter divisions. In this study guide we will use the natural pauses in the narrative to divide the reading into sections. Hence, the first lesson corresponds with the opening expository section of the novel, and thereafter the lessons roughly correspond with Santiago's days at sea.

Page numbers listed after each section title correspond with the page numbers in the Scribner paperback edition of *The Old Man and the Sea*. These page numbers may closely match the page numbers in other editions.

Ideas for Prereading Activities

1. *Map Work:* Locate the country of Cuba on a map. Note Cuba's distance from the United States and the waters surrounding it.

2. *The Lost Generation:* Research American authors and artists from the post-WWI era who were considered part of the "lost generation." Write a one- to two-page paper discussing who these artists were, why they left America, and what they believed regarding life, literature, and art.

3. *Research:* Use an encyclopedia and other sources to find information about deep-sea fishing. Write a one-page paper discussing historical methods of deep-sea fishing.

4. *Courage:* Write a three- to five-paragraph essay discussing how you think people can have courage in the midst of trying circumstances. Consider both personal experience and the Bible when supporting your ideas.

5. Ernest Hemingway is known for his crisp, journalistic approach in writing short stories and novels. As you read *The Old Man and the Sea,* pay close attention to how Hemingway's style contributes to characterization, imagery, and action.

Exposition

(Pages 9–25)

"He was an old man who fished alone in a skiff in the Gulf Stream
and he had gone eighty-four days now without taking a fish."

Vocabulary:

The following underlined words are from sentences in the book. Define each word from the context of the sentence first, and then write the meaning from the dictionary.

1. He always went down to help him carry either the coiled lines or the gaff and harpoon and the sail that was <u>furled</u> around the mast.
   Your Definition:

   Dictionary Definition:

2. The old man was thin and <u>gaunt</u> with deep wrinkles in the back of his neck.
   Your Definition:

   Dictionary Definition:

3. The brown blotches of the <u>benevolent</u> skin cancer the sun brings from its reflection on the tropic sea were on his cheeks.
   Your Definition:

   Dictionary Definition:

4. But none of these scars were fresh. They were as old as <u>erosions</u> in a fishless desert.
   Your Definition:

   Dictionary Definition:

5. "I may not be as strong as I think. . . But I know many tricks and I have <u>resolution</u>."
   Your Definition:

   Dictionary Definition:

Characterization:

1. From the very first paragraph of *The Old Man and the Sea,* the author begins telling us about the two main characters. Read the first paragraph of the novel again. What do we learn about Santiago, the old man, and Manolin, the boy, in this paragraph?

   Santiago:

   Manolin:

2. The second and third paragraphs continue with a physical description of Santiago. Which of Santiago's traits does the second paragraph emphasize? What contrast is drawn with the third paragraph? How do the author's descriptions sharpen the contrast?

3. The description of Santiago's home also gives us information about his character. Read again the description of Santiago's home. What do we learn about Santiago from this description?

Questions:

1. A story's plot is the action of the story. A plot includes an *exposition, rising action, climax, falling action,* and a *resolution.* The *exposition* of a story establishes the setting, introduces characters, and introduces the initial *conflict* or problem. What is the initial conflict or problem introduced in the exposition of *The Old Man and the Sea?*

2. Why did the boy's parents say he couldn't fish with Santiago any longer?

3. How do the other fishermen treat Santiago?

4. Santiago has caught no fish, and has therefore made no money. How has he kept from starving?

Analysis:

5. What is the significance of Santiago's hand scars not being fresh?

6. There are a number of times in *The Old Man and the Sea* where the author draws a parallel between Santiago and Jesus*. For example, the scars on Santiago's hands could be seen as one parallel. Read 1 Peter 2:23. How is Santiago's response to the other fishermen Christ-like?

7. *Foreshadowing* is a literary device used to hint at or suggest something that might happen later in the story. What might the author be foreshadowing with the reminder that Santiago once caught many fish after day 87?

8. What about Joe DiMaggio's heritage makes Santiago relate to him?

* Note: In most cases, when an author draws such parallels, he is trying to create an emotional response to the character based upon our knowledge of Jesus. He is not trying to influence our understanding of Jesus.

9. A *symbol* in literature is something that is used to represent something else. Dreams are often symbolic in literature. Santiago's dreams are never of the present, but only of trips to Africa in his youth. What could these dreams possibly symbolize?

Dig Deeper:

10. Santiago does not seem concerned that he has been labeled "unlucky" by the other fishermen. Instead, he speaks of fishing in terms of "faith" and "doubt." Consider the following conversation between Santiago and the boy:

    > "But remember how you went eighty-seven days without fish and then we caught big ones every day for three weeks."
    > "I remember," the old man said. "I know you did not leave me because you doubted."
    > "It was papa made me leave. I am a boy and I must obey him."
    > "I know," the old man said. "It is quite normal."
    > "He hasn't much faith."
    > "No," the old man said. "But we have. Haven't we?"

    Read Hebrews 11:1. What is given as a definition of "faith" in this verse?

11. What is the "faith" that Santiago and the boy have? On what do they base this faith?

12. When the boy tells Santiago that the Yankees lost, Santiago dismisses it. "That means nothing. The great DiMaggio is himself again."

To Santiago, winning and losing are not of great importance. In regard to Joe DiMaggio and the Yankees, what seems to be important to Santiago? How might this attitude relate to Santiago's own view of success with regard to his fishing?

13. The author writes about Santiago:

He was too simple to wonder when he had attained humility. But he had attained it and he knew it was not disgraceful and it carried no loss of true pride.

Pride and humility are often spoken of as opposites. Here, Hemingway attributes both traits to Santiago. Do you think it is possible to be proud and humble at the same time? Explain your answer.

14. In regard to catching a great fish, Santiago says, "I may not be as strong as I think. . . . But I know many tricks and I have resolution." What is resolution? Where does Santiago get his resolution?

Optional Exercises:

- Research the baseball player Joe DiMaggio and write a one-page essay on his life and career.

First Day at Sea

(Pages 25–53)

"He always thought of the sea as la mar *which is what people call her in Spanish when they love her. . . . The old man always thought of her as feminine and as something that gave or withheld favours. . ."*

Vocabulary:

The words in the left column are taken from the text. Match each word with the best definition found in the right column.

1. ___ condense   a. hook with a handle

2. ___ fathom   b. curl or fold

3. ___ ineffectual   c. compact

4. ___ gelatinous   d. glowing

5. ___ iridescent   e. length equal to six feet

6. ___ gaff   f. to gather into a group or crowd

7. ___ phosphorescence   g. ineffective; inadequate

8. ___ carapaced   h. shifting colors

9. ___ congregate   i. jelly-like

10. ___ furl   j. shielded

Plot:

The following events and/or dialogue happened during Santiago's first day at sea. Number the events in their correct sequence, starting with number "1" as the first event that occurred that day.

a. ____ "*Qué va. . . .* It is what a man must do."

b. ____ Santiago catches a tuna.

c. ____ Santiago puts a sack across his shoulders.

d. ____ Santiago sees a man-of-war bird circling ahead.

e. ____ Santiago sees a Portuguese man-of-war floating beside the boat.

f. ____ The sun rose thinly from the sea and the old man could see the other boats . . .

g. ____ A marlin "nibbles" the bait and leaves.

h. ____ A marlin takes the bait and pulls Santiago for several hours.

i. ____ "Big dolphin."

j. ____ Santiago gets a cut below the eye.

Personification:

1. *Personification* is the attribution of human characteristics to an object, an animal, or an idea. Early in Santiago's voyage out, Hemingway writes that Santiago had always thought of the sea as *la mar,* which is feminine, but that others spoke of the sea as *el mar,* which is masculine. In what ways do Santiago and the other fishermen *personify* the sea?

2. Santiago also attributes human qualities to the marlin he has hooked. List some of the words or phrases Santiago uses to personify the marlin.

Questions:

1. What evidence of Santiago's skill and experience is seen during the first day at sea?

2. What evidence do we see that Santiago is a compassionate man?

3. Santiago lets out his lines with great precision, making sure that each hook is at the exact depth he wants. He considers the difference between being lucky and being exact when fishing. What does he conclude?

4. Santiago catches a small tuna on his first day at sea. What does he intend to do with it?

5. Finally, a marlin begins feeding on Santiago's bait. What does the marlin do when Santiago has set the hook?

6. When the marlin is hooked, why does Santiago continue to hold the line instead of tying the line to the boat?

7. Four times during his first day at sea, Santiago expresses his wish that the boy were with him. Why do you think he wishes this? How does Santiago rebuke himself after the fourth time he expresses this wish?

8. Just before daylight on the second day something takes one of the baits on another one of Santiago's lines. What does Santiago do about it? Why?

Analysis:

9. In literature, a *parallel character* is someone (or something) that has many similarities to the main character and whose purpose is giving further insights into the main character's strengths and/or weaknesses. During Santiago's first day at sea, how might Santiago and the marlin be parallel characters?

Dig Deeper:

10. Early in the first day Santiago admits to himself that he is a precise person in his work and would rather be exact than lucky. Going through the pages of his first day of fishing, give several examples of Santiago's precision in his work. Read 1 Corinthians 10:31; Colossians 3:17, 23; and 1 Thessalonians 4:11, 12. How do these verses say we should work? How do they compare with Santiago's ideas of work?

11. Shortly before Santiago hooks the marlin, he thinks to himself:

    I could just drift . . . and sleep and put a bight of line around my toe to wake me. But today is eighty-five days and I should fish the day well.

What does Santiago's decision tell us about him? Why is it important to Santiago to "fish the day well"? Read Proverbs 10:4; 14:23; 20:13; and 24:33, 34. What is the general idea in these verses? How does this general idea fit with the actions and decisions of Santiago?

12. Given what you've seen so far, write a short description of how you think the story will end and why you think so.

Optional Exercises:

- Twice during his first day at sea, Santiago refers to fishing as "that which I was born for." Have you ever felt that there is something that you are born to do? If so, what is it? What gave you this impression? Write a one-page essay discussing these questions.

- Research information about any of the sea creatures or birds Santiago encounters during his first day at sea. Write a one-page informative essay about that animal.

Second Day at Sea

(Pages 53–86)

Then he was sorry for the great fish that had nothing to eat and his determination to kill him never relaxed in his sorrow for him. How many people will he feed, he thought. But are they worthy to eat him? It is enough to live on the sea and kill our true brothers.

Vocabulary:

A *synonym* is a word that means the same or nearly the same as another word. Read the following sentences from the book. For each of the underlined words, select two synonyms from the word box below.

Word Box

quest	shake	sword	fluctuation
fabricate	surge	blade	invent
	wobble	journey	

1. He was too tired even to examine the line and he <u>teetered</u> on it as his delicate feet gripped it fast.

   _____   _____

2. But what is his plan, he thought. And what is mine? Mine I must <u>improvise</u> to his because of his great size.

   _____   _____

3. He could see the prisms in the deep dark water and the line stretching ahead and the strange <u>undulation</u> of the calm.

_____   _____

4. His sword was as long as a baseball bat and tapered like a <u>rapier</u> and he rose full length from the water and re-entered it . . .

_____   _____

5. ". . . I promise to make a <u>pilgrimage</u> to the Virgin of Cobre if I catch him."

_____   _____

Stream of Consciousness:

1. *Stream of consciousness* is the technique of presenting a narrative as the continuous flow of a character's thoughts and responses. In *The Old Man and the Sea,* once Santiago is alone on the sea, his inner thoughts and spoken dialogue are presented in stream of consciousness as each idea suggests another.

   For example, consider the paragraph beginning "This is the second day now that I do not know the result of the *juegos,* he thought." In that one paragraph, Santiago's thoughts move from baseball scores, to DiMaggio, to bone spurs, to fighting cocks, to endurance, and finally to wishing he was the marlin.

   Find another passage that demonstrates this style.

2. During Santiago's second day at sea, the stream of consciousness technique becomes more apparent. Why might the author choose to use this technique more frequently at this point in the story?

Questions:

1. Why did Santiago want the marlin to jump?

2. During the first day at sea, we began to see a relationship develop between Santiago and the marlin. How does this relationship deepen on the second day?

3. How does Santiago injure his right hand? What happens to Santiago's left hand?

4. What does Santiago do with the tuna he caught on the previous day?

5. How does the thought of Joe DiMaggio inspire Santiago during the second day at sea?

6. What incident from his past did Santiago call to mind to give himself confidence? Why might this incident give Santiago confidence in his struggle against the marlin?

7. Why did Santiago give up arm-wrestling?

8. Why does Santiago look for a swirl in the water when he throws the carcass of the dolphin overboard?

Analysis:

9. In the last section we discussed parallel characters and listed ways in which Hemingway used Santiago and the marlin as parallel characters. List four more ways we see a parallel drawn between Santiago and the marlin on this second day at sea.

10. Hemingway uses birds to parallel and symbolize different aspects of Santiago's experience. For example, early in his journey out Santiago notices the small birds who "were always flying and looking and almost never finding." This parallels Santiago's experience on the previous 84 days. Then, just prior to Santiago's success in finding and catching the marlin, a man-of-war bird is seen catching fish.

    On Santiago's second day at sea, a tired warbler rests on Santiago's stern. What might the appearance of this bird say about Santiago at this point in the story?

11. Santiago wonders if the warbler is a young warbler who has never crossed the gulf before, and he understands that the warbler will "learn about the hawks soon enough."

    "Take a good rest, small bird," he said. "Then go in and take your chance like any man or bird or fish."

    What general statement does Santiago seem to be making about the process of growing older?

12. Read again the description of the marlin as it leaps from the water. Hemingway does not give specific measurements of the fish (except to say that it is two feet longer than Santiago's boat), but he lets the reader understand the immensity of the fish through the use of descriptive language. Write down the descriptive words or phrases that are used to communicate the size of the fish.

13. At times during the second day at sea, Santiago imagines himself in the position of the marlin he has hooked. "If I were him, I would put in everything now and go until something broke." List two other times Santiago imagines himself in this position.

14. Santiago seems to wish he were the marlin because the marlin possesses certain qualities he admires. What are these qualities? What qualities does Santiago recognize that he himself possesses?

15. In the midst of his fatigue, Santiago thinks, "I wish he'd [the marlin] sleep and I could sleep and dream about the lions. . . . Why are the lions the main thing that is left?" Why do you suppose that the lions are the main thing that Santiago dreams about?

16. Before Santiago dreams of the lions, he has two other dreams. What are these dreams and what might they symbolize?

Dig Deeper:

17. At the beginning of his struggle against the marlin, Santiago makes little acknowledgment of or reference to God. Now, as his second day begins, Santiago says "God let him [the marlin] jump." Later he says "God help me to have the cramp go." Finally he makes promises to God. What does he promise to do if he catches the fish?

18. On the second day at sea, Santiago makes a vow to God. Read Numbers 30:1, 2; Deuteronomy 23:21–23; Ecclesiastes 5:4–6; Matthew 5:33–37; and James 5:12. What do these verses say about making vows to God and making vows in general? What difference do you see between the Old Testament verses and the New Testament verses? Why do you think they differ?

19. Though we have not seen Santiago pray or talk to God before, suddenly we see him talking to God and saying prayers a number of times. Why do you think this is? Read Philippians 4:6, 7; Colossians 4:2; 1 Thessalonians 5:16–18. How do these verses say we should pray? Is Santiago doing this? Give an example of how you could do this in your daily routine.

20. As noted earlier, Santiago finds ways to encourage himself in the midst of difficulty. Read Psalm 94:18,19, Lamentations 3:21–24, and Hebrews 10:23–25. What can Christians do to encourage themselves in the midst of difficulty?

Optional Exercises:

- *Using Stream-of-Consciousness:* Recall an important incident or event from your life. As you think about it, pay attention to how your thoughts and actions flow together in a continuous stream. Write a one-page narrative relating the incident using the stream-of-consciousness technique.

- Read the following passage and then draw or paint a picture of the scene.

   A small bird came toward the skiff from the north. He was a warbler and flying very low over the water . . . . The bird made the stern of the boat and rested there. Then he flew around the old man's head and rested on the line where he was more comfortable.
   "How old are you?" the old man asked the bird. "Is this your first trip?"

- Write a poem describing the marlin's journey in the sea or relating events from the marlin's limited point of view.

Third Day at Sea

(Pages 86–122)

With his [the marlin's] mouth shut and his tail straight up and down we sail like brothers.
Then his head started to become a little unclear and he thought, is he bringing me in
or am I bringing him in? . . . . But they were sailing together lashed side by side
and the old man thought, let him bring me in if it pleases him.
I am only better than him through trickery and he meant me no harm.

Vocabulary:

Read each of the sentences below, paying close attention to the use of the underlined word. Then write down the definition of each underlined word according to how it is being used.

1. He just felt a faint slackening of the pressure of the line and he <u>commenced</u> to pull on it gently with his right hand.

2. His old legs and shoulders <u>pivoted</u> with the swinging of the pulling.

3. On each calm <u>placid</u> turn the fish made he was gaining line and he was sure that in two more turns he would have a chance to get the harpoon in.

4. . . . the fish pulled part way over and then <u>righted</u> himself and swam away.

5. He cut the rope then and went <u>astern</u> to noose the tail.

6. He had come up from deep down in the water as the dark cloud of blood had settled and <u>dispersed</u> in the mile deep sea.

7. . . . he rammed the harpoon down onto the shark's head at a spot where the line between his eyes <u>intersected</u> with the line that ran straight back from his nose.

8. The water was white where his tail beat it and three-quarters of his body was clear above the water when the rope came <u>taut</u>, shivered, and then snapped.

9. They were hateful sharks, bad smelling, <u>scavengers</u> as well as killers, and when they were hungry they would bite at an oar or the rudder of a boat.

10. He did not want to think of the <u>mutilated</u> under-side of the fish.

Questions:

1. As the marlin begins to circle, Santiago makes yet another promise to God in exchange for the strength to help him endure. What promise does he make? Does he keep this promise?

2. Earlier, Santiago wanted the marlin to jump. Why doesn't he want the marlin to jump now?

3. Why does Santiago try to get the marlin in close to the boat?

4. What physical symptoms does Santiago experience while bringing the marlin in?

5. Santiago guesses that the marlin is over 1,500 pounds and might "dress out two thirds of that at thirty cents a pound." Do the math for Santiago: how much money would the marlin earn him? Why is this amount of money so significant?

6. Although the sharks take his fish, Santiago blames himself for its loss. What error does he tell himself (and the fish) that he made?

Analysis:

7. Out on the sea, Santiago ponders many things, and often speaks aloud. On the third day as Santiago reaches the limit of his exhaustion, his thoughts and his words have a different tone from that on the previous two days. Explain the difference.

8. While talking to himself on the third day, Santiago often contradicts himself or rebukes himself for the things he says.

    > I must get him alongside this time, he thought. I am not good for many more turns. Yes, you are, he told himself. You're good for ever.

    > The dentuso is cruel and able and strong and intelligent. But I was more intelligent than he was. Perhaps not, he thought. Perhaps I was only better armed.

    > Besides, he thought, everything kills everything else in some way. Fishing kills me exactly as it keeps me alive. The boy keeps me alive, he thought. I must not deceive myself too much.

    What "opposing sides" can we see emerging in Santiago's conversations with himself? How would you define the two "sides" of Santiago's conversations?

9. After Santiago ties the marlin to the side of the boat, the author writes:

   > With his mouth shut and his tail straight up and down we sail like brothers. Then his head started to become a little unclear and he thought, is he bringing me in or am I bringing him in?

   What might this passage symbolize or reinforce about Santiago's relationship with the marlin?

10. As Santiago starts to sail homeward with the marlin tied to the boat, he keeps glancing at the fish to assure himself that it really is true. Readers can almost feel Santiago's incredulous joy. At this point in the narrative when everything seems to have worked out in Santiago's favor, Hemingway ends a paragraph with the following sentence: "It was an hour before the first shark hit him." What effect does this sentence, and its placement in the narrative, have on the reader?

11. List each weapon Santiago uses to fend off the sharks, and how each weapon is lost or rendered useless. How does Santiago respond to the sharks when his last weapon is gone? What does this response indicate about Santiago?

12. Santiago wonders if it was a sin to kill the marlin. What reasons does he give for killing the marlin? How does he justify killing the shark?

13. While Santiago was in battle with the marlin, he often spoke to the marlin. Now, as the sharks continue to take pieces of the marlin, Santiago no longer talks to the marlin or even looks at him. What might explain this change?

14. As he sails homeward, Santiago begins to talk of luck:

> I have half of [the fish], he thought. Maybe I'll have the luck to bring the forward half in. I should have some luck. No, he said. You violated your luck when you went too far outside.
>
> "Don't be silly," he said aloud. "And keep awake and steer. You may have much luck yet.
>
> "I'd like to buy some if there's any place they sell it," he said.

How has Santiago's view of luck changed? What might this change indicate about Santiago's view of himself?

15. As Santiago nears the harbor, he thinks about his boat:

> She's good, he thought. She is sound and not harmed in any way except for the tiller. That is easily replaced.

What does this passage indicate about Santiago's plans for the future?

Dig Deeper:

16. As he faces the loss of his marlin, Santiago wonders if it is a sin to not have hope. Do you think it is a sin to not have hope?

17. As Santiago prepares for the attack of the first shark, he was "full of resolution but he had little hope." What is the difference between resolution and hope? Why would someone have resolution if he has no hope? Have you ever been in a situation in which you had resolution but little hope?

18. While he is sailing, waiting for the sharks to attack, Santiago begins to think about sin. Beginning with the paragraph that starts, "It is silly not to hope, he thought. Besides, I believe it is a sin," read the next page or so. Judging from these paragraphs, how does Santiago seem to define and view sin? What does Santiago seem to think about sin? Read Matthew 5:17–48, Mark 7:18–23, James 4:17. From these verses, how would you define sin?

19. After the first shark attacks, Santiago says, "A man can be destroyed, but not defeated." What do you think he means by this? Do you agree? Look also at Matthew 10:28.

Optional Exercises:

- Consider Santiago's hopes and failures at sea. Why do you think God allows difficult things to happen to people who work hard and have faith? Write a personal essay about a time in your life when God brought you through a difficult situation.

Resolution

(Pages 122–127)

Up the road, in his shack, the old man was sleeping again. He was still sleeping on his face and the boy was sitting by him watching him. The old man was dreaming about the lions.

Questions:

1. What does Manolin do after he sees that Santiago has returned?

2. How long was the marlin?

3. Who is Santiago talking about when he tells Manolin, "They beat me."

4. How does Santiago respond when Manolin announces that he will fish with Santiago again? How does Santiago's response indicate a change in his view of himself as a fisherman?

Analysis:

5. One necessary characteristic of either a student or a disciple is to be teachable. What evidence is there in the concluding pages of the story that Manolin is teachable?

6. When Santiago returns to his shack and falls asleep, Hemingway says, "he slept face down on the newspapers with his arms out straight and the palms of his hands up." Hemingway does not say whether Santiago's arms are out straight over his head or straight out from his sides. As an experiment, lie down on your bed or the floor and try both positions. Which do you think is the position in which Santiago was lying? What symbolism could be attached to the way in which Santiago was lying?

7. Why does Santiago lay with his hands palms up? Why does Manolin cry when he sees Santiago's hands?

8. Why do you think Manolin is determined now to go fishing with Santiago?

9. What do the final scenes tell us about Santiago's situation and his future? Does this leave you with a positive or negative impression?

10. Quickly review the early pages of *The Old Man and the Sea* and note how Santiago was treated by other fishermen and villagers. Have their attitudes changed toward him at the end of the novel? Give evidence to explain your answer.

11. Some critics have drawn a parallel between Santiago and the marlin. At the end of the story, the marlin is reduced to "the long backbone of the great fish that was now just garbage waiting to go out with the tide." Do you think this is how Santiago should be viewed also? Why?

Optional Exercises:

- Santiago's strength and encouragement often come from his dreams of youth. Write a narrative poem about Santiago's dreams of the lions on the white beaches of Africa.

Overview

1. Conflict is the struggle between opposing forces that forms the basis of the plot in narrative literature. Conflict can be organized into the following forms:

    *   man vs. man
    *   man vs. his environment (nature, society, etc.)
    *   man vs. himself

    In *The Old Man and the Sea,* do you think Santiago's greatest conflict is against his environment or against himself? Explain your reasoning.

2. The *climax* of a story is the highest point of action and tension. It is also the turning point of the story which sets in motion the eventual conclusion of the plot's central conflict. What is the climax of *The Old Man and the Sea?*

3. In the *resolution* of a story, all plot complications are finally sorted out, the conflict is solved, and the story is brought to a conclusion. One characteristic of the modernist style is that works are often fragmented, with little or no resolution. Does *The Old Man and the Sea* have a resolution? If so, do you find it to be a satisfying conclusion to the story? Explain your answers.

4. A *theme* is the main idea or message that is communicated through a work of literature. It might also be called the lesson about life an author hopes to share with his readers. Theme can be discovered in many ways: by observing character growth and change; by evaluating conflict and resolution; by evaluating symbolism; by paying attention to ideas and details that are repeated; and by paying attention to the author's tone and style.

    What do you think is the primary theme of *The Old Man and the Sea*? Give a few examples of how this is expressed in the novel.

5. What do you think are some minor themes found in the novel?

6. Main characters often change over the course of a novel. Characters that change are called *dynamic* characters. Characters that remain the same are called *static* characters. Is Santiago a dynamic or static character? If dynamic, how has Santiago changed?

7. Earlier in the novel we discussed the possible parallels between Santiago and Christ. One clear example occurs when Santiago makes a noise at the sight of two more sharks. The author says that "it is just a noise such as a man might make, involuntarily, feeling the nail go through his hands and into the wood." Later, after Santiago has returned home, the author writes:

    > Then he shouldered the mast and started to climb [the hill]. It was then he knew the depth of his tiredness. He stopped for a moment and looked back . . . He started to climb again and at the top he fell and lay for some time with the mast across his shoulder. He tried to get up. But it was too difficult . . .

    Many literary scholars believe this passage is also an allusion to Christ. In what way might this passage draw a parallel between Santiago and Christ?

8. In literature a character is referred to as a *Christ figure* if that character's suffering or death accomplishes a great task or has a redemptive effect. Do you see any sort of accomplishment or redemption through Santiago's suffering? Explain your answer. Given the outcome of the novel, do you think Hemingway's use of Santiago as a Christ figure is justified?

9. The *hero* is the central character, or *protagonist* in a work of literature. The traditional hero possesses positive qualities which help him triumph in the novel's main conflict. A *tragic hero* is a protagonist who possesses a character flaw which ultimately causes his downfall. An *anti-hero* is a protagonist who does not possess the positive qualities of the traditional hero. According to these definitions, do you think Santiago is a traditional hero, a tragic hero, or an anti-hero? Explain your answer.

10. While he is battling the marlin, and later as he fights the sharks, Santiago begins to blame himself for the way things begin to go wrong, saying he went out too far. Looking back over the novel, who do you think is to blame for the way things turned out? Are bad things always the fault of someone? Read Ecclesiastes 9:11 and address it in your answer.

11. *The Old Man and the Sea* begins and ends with the relationship between Santiago and Manolin. Even while he is in the boat, far out at sea, Santiago repeatedly thinks about the boy. Describe the relationship between the old man and the boy and the conflict they have to deal with. Read Ecclesiastes 4:9–12. How do these verses relate to some of the problems Santiago has at sea and how these are resolved at the end of the novel?

12. In an earlier section we looked at the following verses regarding Santiago and how he worked: Proverbs 10:4, Proverbs 14:23, and Proverbs 20:13. Although Santiago seems to follow these verses, he does not receive the benefits promised. The same may be said for many people. How do you account for this? Read also Ecclesiastes 9:11. How do you reconcile these two viewpoints?

Essays

Choose two of the following topics and write a one- to two-page essay.

1. Discuss the distinct characteristics of Hemingway's narrative style, including his arrangement of narrative description and limited dialogue in *The Old Man and the Sea*. Compare Hemingway's style to that of other writers you may enjoy. Share your opinion of Hemingway's methods and techniques.

2. Throughout *The Old Man and the Sea*, Santiago talks to himself and gives himself advice, some of it as simple statements, such as, "Every day is a new day," or "It is better to be lucky. But I would rather be exact. Then when luck comes you are ready." These could easily be considered proverbs such as Benjamin Franklin wrote in *Poor Richard's Almanack*. Gather 10–25 of Santiago's statements together in a list called something like *Santiago's Proverbs* or *Santiago's Sayings*. If you wish, add your own comments or interpretations next to the sayings.

3. Write an essay discussing the use of Christian imagery and allusions in *The Old Man and the Sea*. Identify examples of Christian imagery and allusions and the contributions they give to the novel. Address why Hemingway might have used these images and allusions and why he was trying to say with them.

4. Use a dictionary to research the definitions of "discourage" and "encourage." Write an essay clarifying the meanings of these words and discussing factors found in the novel that both encourage and discourage Santiago.

5. Consider the outcome of *The Old Man and the Sea*. Is the novel an optimistic story of human victory or a pessimistic story of defeat?

6. At least four times Santiago expresses that he wishes catching the marlin had only been a dream. The question he raises is perhaps the central question of the novel: is it better to have achieved something only to have it taken away or to have never achieved it at all? What do you think? What answer does Hemingway supply in his novel?

Additional Resources

Other Books by Ernest Hemingway:

Novels:

Across the River and Into the Trees	published by Scribner
A Farewell to Arms	published by Scribner
For Whom the Bell Tolls	published by Scribner
The Garden of Eden	published by Scribner
Islands in the Stream	published by Scribner
The Sun Also Rises	published by Scribner
To Have and Have Not	published by Scribner

Short Fiction:

The Complete Short Stories	published by Scribner
The Fifth Column, and Four Stories of the Spanish Civil War	published by Scribner
In Our Time	published by Scribner
Men Without Women	published by Scribner
The Nick Adams Stories	published by Macmillan
The Snows of Kilimanjaro, and Other Stories	published by Scribner
Winner Take Nothing	published by Macmillan

Non-fiction:

The Dangerous Summer	published by Touchstone Books
Death in the Afternoon	published by Scribner

Green Hills of Africa	published by Touchstone Books
A Moveable Feast	published by Touchstone Books

Books of Related Interest:

Captains Courageous	by Rudyard Kipling, various publishers
Moby Dick	by Herman Melville, various publishers
The Open Boat	by Stephen Crane, various publishers
The Perfect Storm	by Sebastian Junger, published by HarperCollins
South Sea Tales	by Jack London, published by Mutual Publishing Company

Films:

The Old Man and the Sea (1958)	Starring Spencer Tracy.
Moby Dick (1956)	Starring Gregory Peck, Orson Welles, and Richard Basehart
Moby Dick (1998)	Starring Patrick Stewart, Gregory Peck, and Henry Thomas

Answer Key

Exposition
Vocabulary:

1. wrapped or rolled; 2. thin and angular; 3. kind or generous; 4. land worn away by water, wind, or ice; 5. will or determination

Characterization:

1. <u>Santiago</u>: We are told that he is old, he fishes alone, and that he has not caught a fish for 84 days. We are told that he is considered "salao, which is the worst form of unlucky." As if to reinforce this, the author ends the paragraph by saying that the old man's sail looks like "the flag of permanent defeat." <u>Manolin</u>: We know right away that the boy cares for the old man. He had fished with Santiago until his parents had ordered him to go in another boat. He feels sad when he sees the old man come in each day with no fish. Even though he is not fishing with Santiago, he helps Santiago carry all of his gear.

2. The second paragraph emphasizes Santiago's age. The third paragraph contrasts this by telling us that everything about Santiago is old "except his eyes." The effect is heightened by the use of contrasting descriptions. In the second paragraph, Santiago's scars are described as being "as old as erosions in a fishless desert." But his eyes are described as being "the same color as the sea, . . . cheerful and undefeated." The contrast between these descriptions—one dry and fishless, the other being the sea (and presumably full of fish)—shows the sharp contrast between Santiago's outward appearance and something within him which remains young.

3. Santiago's home is just a shack. The mast of his skiff is nearly as long as the one room of the shack. Inside there is just a bed, a table, a chair, and a place on the dirt floor for cooking. The sparseness of the shack suggests that Santiago may spend most of his time fishing on the sea. It also speaks of Santiago's poverty, but may also hint at a simplicity of spirit—a man who does not desire many things. There is no food (and we know that Santiago has not caught any fish) so Santiago must be supported by others, specifically the boy and the man who gives the boy food and beer. We learn that Santiago was married, but that he will not display the picture of his wife because it makes him feel lonely. The two pictures that he does display suggests that Santiago is (or at least his wife was) Catholic.

Questions:

1. The initial conflict or problem introduced in the exposition is that Santiago has not caught a fish for 84 days.

2. The boy's parents told him he couldn't fish with Santiago any longer because Santiago had gone to sea 40 days without catching a fish. This was "salao, which is the worst form of unlucky."

3. Some of the other fishermen make fun of Santiago. However, the older men look at Santiago with sadness. They seem to have pity for him.

4. The boy has taken it upon himself to make sure that Santiago has food to eat. Also, it appears that another man in the village, Martin, is helping by giving food to the boy to give to Santiago.

Analysis:

5. The fact that Santiago's scars have healed reminds the reader that it has been a long time since Santiago last brought in a fish.

6. When he is insulted by the other fishermen, Santiago makes no reply.

7. The reminder that Santiago once caught many fish after day 87 foreshadows that Santiago might catch fish soon.

8. Santiago relates to Joe DiMaggio because DiMaggio's father was a fisherman.

9. Answers may vary. Santiago's dreams possibly symbolize that he is living in the past, or that he has not lost the faith and courage of his youth. These dreams, like Santiago's eyes, are a part of Santiago that remains young.

Dig Deeper:

10. This passage defines faith as "being sure of what we hope for, and certain of what we do not see."

11. They have faith that Santiago will catch a fish. This is not based on superstition about luck, but rather on Santiago's skill as a fisherman.

12. Answers may vary. What seems to be most important to Santiago are the great skills of the individual players on the team. Even if his favorite team loses, Santiago admires how DiMaggio plays. Similarly, we can see that it does not matter to Santiago if he was "unlucky" in fishing. He knows that he has the skill to bring in fish, and that is all that seems to matter to him.

13. Answers will vary. It may depend on the student's definition of pride—whether it is limited to inflated regard for oneself and the demand for attention from others or whether pride can also be regarded as self respect and accurate appreciation of one's abilities.

14. Answers may vary. Resolution is courage or determination. Santiago gets his resolution from his confidence in his skill as a fisherman.

First Day at Sea
Vocabulary:
1. c; 2. e; 3. g; 4. i; 5. h; 6. a; 7. d; 8. j; 9. f; 10. b
Plot:
a. 1; b. 6; c. 9; d. 3; e. 5; f. 2; g. 7; h. 8; i. 4; j. 10
Personification:
1. Santiago thought of the sea as something that gave or withheld favors, could be cruel or wild and wicked, and sometimes could not help itself. Others thought of the sea as a contestant, or an enemy.

2. Santiago muses that the fish may be "too wise to jump"; he wonders if the marlin "has any plans" or if he is "just as desperate as I am"; he says it was necessary for the marlin "to make a choice" to stay in the deep water.
Questions:
1. Santiago's skill is seen in how he baits his hooks and sets his lines, how he reads the signals from the birds and other fish to tell him that larger fish are around, and how he catches and handles the marlin.

2. Santiago shows compassion in the way he feels sorry for the small terns that were "always flying and looking and almost never finding," in the way he compares himself to the turtles ("I have such a heart too and my feet and hands are like theirs"), and in the pity he begins to feel for the marlin he has hooked.

3. Santiago says that that it is better to be lucky, but that he would rather be exact, because then, when luck comes, he will be ready for it and able to take advantage of it.

4. Santiago intends to use it for bait.

5. The marlin barely reacts. Instead, it moves off steadily and slowly through the water, towing Santiago and his boat behind him.

6. Had Santiago tied the line to the boat, the marlin might have broken it. But by holding onto the line, Santiago can allow slack when it is necessary, and pull it in when he needs to, depending on the movements of the fish.

7. Santiago wishes that the boy were there to help him bring in the marlin. He also wishes that the boy could see the marlin, but it is likely that Santiago mainly wishes for the companionship of the boy. The fourth time Santiago reminds himself that he only has himself, so he had better do what needs to be done.

8. Santiago cuts the line, then cuts the other two lines. He does not want to be distracted from his task, and he does not want the other lines to tangle with the marlin. The lines, hooks, and leaders Santiago loses can be replaced; the marlin he has hooked cannot.
Analysis:
9. Answers may vary. There are many times when Santiago and the marlin are paralleled through Santiago's actions and thoughts. Early in the day, Santiago thinks that the struggle will kill the fish. "He [the fish] can't do this forever." The reader also wonders if the struggle will also kill Santiago. Later, as the marlin shows no sign of tiring, Santiago thinks "I can do nothing with him and he can do nothing with me." Santiago wonders if the fish "has any plans or if he is just as desperate as I am." Santiago also connects them through the choices they have made, and through their isolation from everything else. "His choice had been to stay in the deep dark water . . . . My choice was to go there and find him . . . . Now we are joined together and have been since noon. And no one to help either one of us." Santiago wonders if the fish's back feels "as badly as mine." Finally, Santiago says to the fish, "I'll stay with you until I am dead."
Dig Deeper:
10. Answers will vary. Some examples of Santiago's precision include keeping his lines clear and at their proper depths, using the bird to find fish, the patience and care he showed when hooking the marlin, not tying the marlin's line to the boat, using the sack to protect his back, etc. The verses speak favorably of work and working with our hands, but particularly of doing everything with all our heart and for God, implying that everything should be done to the best of our ability. Santiago's ideas appear very similar, though without the emphasis on God.

11. Answer will vary. Some possibilities are that Santiago is persistent and conscientious. He knows that slackening his attention and work can lead to sloppiness and missed opportunity. The general idea of the verses is something like, "to succeed you must work hard." This seems to fit well with the way Santiago behaves.

12. Answers will vary.

Second Day at Sea
Vocabulary:

1. wobble; shake; 2. invent; fabricate; 3. surge; fluctuation; 4. sword; blade; 5. journey; quest

Stream of Consciousness:

1. Answers will vary. Accept reasonable responses. Some examples include the following: The paragraph that begins "Now that he had seen him once, he could picture the fish swimming in the water. . . ." The paragraph that begins "It must be very strange to be in an airplane, he thought." The paragraphs that begin "'The fish is my friend, too,' he said aloud."

2. The use of this technique helps communicate how fatigued Santiago is becoming. As he grows more tired, his thoughts grow more disjointed. This becomes even more apparent on Santiago's third day at sea.

Questions:

1. If the marlin jumped, its sacks would fill with air and it would not be able to go deep.

2. Santiago begins to speak of the marlin as a "friend" and a "brother." He tells the fish that he loves and respects him. He expresses sorrow for the fish.

3. Early in the day the marlin lurches, and Santiago's right hand is cut by the line. Later, his left hand cramps up and becomes useless.

4. Instead of using it for bait as he had intended, Santiago decides to eat it to give himself strength.

5. Santiago is inspired with thoughts of DiMaggio, because DiMaggio has the courage to play baseball even though he suffers from a bone spur. DiMaggio's courage in the midst of suffering inspires Santiago to persevere during the difficult night.

6. To give himself confidence, Santiago recalls the arm-wrestling contest in which he defeated "the strongest man on the docks" after a 24-hour struggle. Answers will vary. It would remind Santiago that if he doesn't give up his struggle, and continues to persevere, he will bring in the fish.

7. Santiago decided that he could beat anyone if he wanted to badly enough. He also decided that it was bad for his right hand for fishing, and fishing was apparently more important to him than winning at arm wrestling.

8. The swirl would indicate that sharks were nearby.

Analysis:

9. Answers will vary. When the fish lurches and Santiago is cut by the line, Santiago says that something hurt the marlin to make him lurch. Both are apparently injured at the same time. When Santiago begins to eat, he wishes to feed the marlin, too. As Santiago wonders what the marlin's plan is, he wonders what his own plan is, and he realizes that the plans of one depend on the plans made by the other. Santiago wonders if the fish jumped to show himself to Santiago. He then expresses a desire to show himself to the marlin. After he prays "Holy Mary, Mother of God, pray for us sinners now and at the hour of our death," he immediately adds "Blessed Virgin, pray for the death of this fish." Santiago recalls telling the boy that he was "a strange old man." A few paragraphs later he remarks that the fish "must be very strange."

10. Answers may vary. The tired warbler possibly symbolizes Santiago's exhaustion and need for rest.

11. Youth has relatively few worries, perhaps because the young do not understand everything about the struggles one will face in life. Santiago is suggesting that facing trials is part of what comes with maturity. The warbler does not know about the hawks and does not concern itself with them because it is young, but it will learn about the hawks in due time.

12. The fish came out of the water "unendingly." Water "poured from his sides." His sword "was as long as a baseball bat and tapered like a rapier." His tail was like a "great scythe-blade."

13. After the fish jumps, Santiago thinks, "I wish I was the fish, . . . with everything he has against only my will and my intelligence." Later he thinks, "Man is not much beside the great birds and beasts. Still I would rather be that beast down there in the darkness of the sea."

14. To the marlin, Santiago attributes nobility, ability, greatness, brute strength, dignity. To himself Santiago attributes strength of will and intelligence.

15. Answers may vary. The lions represent Santiago's youth when his life was simple and carefree. Santiago may be unconsciously longing for his simple youth again, or the lions symbolize the strength and carefree power Santiago apparently once had.

16. First, Santiago dreams of "a vast school of porpoises that stretched for eight or ten miles." Then he dreams he is back in the village on his bed, that he is cold, and that his arm is asleep because he had been resting his head on it. Answers may vary. The dream of the porpoises that stretch for eight or ten miles may represent the distance that Santiago is from shore. The dream of lying on his bed with his arm being asleep may represent Santiago's extreme fatigue, and the fact that his arm is especially fatigued by holding the line tight. More figurative interpretations may be that the dolphins represent the vigor of Santiago's youth and the second dream of cold and sleep may represent his age and physical deterioration.

Dig Deeper:

17. He promises to make a pilgrimage to the Virgin of Cobre.

18. The verses say it is dangerous to make a promise or vow to God, but if you do so you had better fulfill it. Most of the verses say it is unwise to swear by something or make a vow at all. Answers will vary. The Old Testament verses discourage the making of vows, but say if someone makes one he must follow through or fall into sin. The New Testament verses simply say not to make vows or swear by something. In essence they say nothing more should be needed than to say "yes" or "no." This may be because a vow such as Santiago makes is too close to trying to manipulate God by bargaining with God, or it may be because we cannot foresee or control the future and what may happen or what may actually be demanded of us. For a pledge or vow gone terribly wrong, see Judges 11:29–40.

19. Answer may vary for all questions. Santiago, like many people, may not pray until he feels rather desperate, or he may use prayer like a "lucky charm," thrown in for good measure. Many people, when they feel they've done all they can or when they feel uncertain, turn to God in prayer. These verses say we should be praying about everything, devotedly, and continually. In a sense Santiago is doing some of this—as things happen this day he brings them up to God. Santiago also offers formal, ritual prayer to God. These verses appear to be referring to more of a respectful conversational prayer to God, offering requests, concerns, and thankfulness throughout the day.

20. Answers may vary. In the midst of difficulty, Christians can remind themselves of God's love and faithfulness, and we can turn to fellow Christians for strength and encouragement.

Third Day at Sea

Vocabulary:

1. began; started; 2. turned; 3. quiet; serene; 4. leveled; straightened; 5. toward the back of the boat; 6. dissipated; spread out; 7. met; crossed; 8. tight; tense; 9. an animal that feeds on dead animals or refuse; 10. torn; shredded

Questions:

1. Santiago promises to "say a hundred Our Fathers and a hundred Hail Marys." Later, as he loses the marlin to the sharks, he remembers his promise, but says that he is too tired to pray. This is a good example of why we are warned to not make bargains with God—in our weakness we too often fail to follow through.

2. Santiago is afraid that if the marlin jumps it might throw the hook and escape.

3. Santiago wants to get the marlin close to the boat so he can kill it with the harpoon.

4. While bringing the marlin in, Santiago sees black spots, feels faint, gets confused, and feels nauseous.

5. The marlin would earn approximately $300.00. $300.00 is very significant to Santiago, who lived at a time when the U.S. minimum wages (which were higher than those of Cuba) were set at 25 cents per hour, or $520 per year. $300.00 would change Santiago's life.

6. Santiago says that he went too far out to fish, and for that reason he failed. He even says "You violated your luck when you went too far outside."

Analysis:

7. Early in his journey when Santiago begins talking to himself his conversation tends to reflect the things he sees or experiences. Later, his spoken words express his deeper pondering about humanity and nature. During this time he tends to speak to the fish. On the last day, his thoughts reflect his inner struggles and emotions.

8. One of Santiago's "voices" appears to take a negative, often accusatory view, while the other attempts to encourage Santiago with a more positive view, often justifying his actions.

9. This passage might symbolize Santiago's reliance on nature to succeed. It might also symbolize that in the end, ironically, although Santiago killed the marlin, he is still dependent on the marlin for survival. The passage also reinforces the bond Santiago has with the marlin. Santiago continues to identify with the marlin to the point of considering the marlin an equal. He says, "I am only better than him through trickery and he meant me no harm." Had Santiago been towing the marlin behind, or if the marlin had been in the boat, the marlin would have lost "dignity." Santiago seems to prefer that they sail homeward side by side.

10. By slipping this sentence in almost casually at the end of a paragraph, Hemingway mimics the suddenness and surprise of the shark attack. As Santiago realizes that the tide of fortune has turned against him, the reader begins to suspect the inevitability of Santiago's loss.

11. First, Santiago uses his harpoon, but loses the harpoon in a shark. Then he fixes his knife to an oar, but the knife breaks. Then he beats the sharks with the oar, using it as a club. But in the darkness, a shark takes the oar. Finally, he rips out the tiller and uses that as a club, eventually breaking it. Even then he takes a few last stabs with the splintered end of the tiller. After that, when the sharks come for the last of the marlin, Santiago pays no attention to them. This indicates that he has accepted the inevitable: he will not bring home the fish.

12. Santiago says that he killed the marlin "to keep me alive and to feed many people." Then he adds that he "killed him for pride and because you were a fisherman." Santiago says that he killed the shark in self-defense.

13. Answers will vary. Santiago may not want to acknowledge the loss of the fish, or to see his success taken from him. He often says that it would have been better if it had been a dream. There is something in Santiago that does not want to face the reality of the situation. He admired and respected the fish and he does not want to see it ravaged.

14. Earlier, Santiago expressed faith that he would catch a fish based not on luck, but on his skills as a fisherman. Even as he lets down his lines, he says "It is better to be lucky, but I would rather be exact." Now he seems willing to trade anything for just a bit of luck. "I would take some [luck] in any form and pay what they asked." This may indicate that Santiago is struggling with self-doubt.

15. Santiago intends to keep fishing. His great loss has not caused him to give it up completely.

Dig Deeper:

16. Answers will vary. To have lost hope that a certain thing will happen probably is not a sin. But to have lost hope in life, to feel totally deserted or helpless, certainly is a dangerous position to be in. Whether it is a sin or not, it is a point at which one's faith in God has failed. A number of the Psalms address this feeling of hopelessness, as does Elijah's experience in 1 Kings 19:1–18.

17. Answers will vary. To be resolute is to be full of determination; hope is the anticipation or confidence of success or a satisfactory result. Some may say there is no point to be resolute without hope. Other answers may be that a person should be resolute when he knows he is in the right, or when you simply should finish the job. Accept reasonable answers. Personal answers will vary.

18. Answers will vary. Santiago seems to want to avoid the subject of sin because he does not have a good grasp of what it is and in what way he might be guilty. He says he has "no understanding of it and I am not sure that I believe in it." Then he seems concerned that "everything is a sin." He decides someone else should figure it out. In the verses listed there are several elements to sin. First, there is violation of the basic law given in the Old Testament, the 10 Commandments. But Jesus also broadens it by saying that our attitudes and motives can also be sin. Sin comes from the anger, lust, deceit, etc., in our hearts, even if we don't commit the "big" sins. James expands it even more by saying it is a sin to know good but not to do it. It is this question of motives and attitudes that probably confuses Santiago. Answers will vary. You may wish to share these verses with students: Romans 3:20–24, James 1:13–16, 1 John 1:7–2:1.

19. Answers will vary. Santiago may be saying something similar to Matthew 10:28. Others can damage or destroy our bodies, but only we can determine what happens to our true inner self. Matthew 10:28 points out that only we and God determine who we really are and where we spend eternity.

Resolution

Questions:

1. After Manolin sees that Santiago has returned he looks at Santiago's hands and cries. He then goes to get some coffee for Santiago.

2. The marlin measured 18 feet from nose to tail.

3. Santiago says the sharks beat him.

4. Santiago at first says no, that he is no longer lucky. He also expresses concern over what Manolin's family will say. Santiago's view of himself seems to have suffered by the end of the novel.

Analysis:

5. It is evident that Manolin is teachable because he tells Santiago "I still have much to learn," and later says, "there is much that I can learn and you can teach me everything."

6. Answers will vary. Face down with the arms out to the side seems awkward but it is the most obvious choice. It could symbolize the crucified Christ and tie in with Santiago's carrying his mast up the hill on his shoulders. Santiago also may have slept with his arms laid out above his head. This position is more reminiscent of a supplicant asking for mercy or favor. Both symbols fit in with the character and the story.

7. Santiago's hand are badly damaged; a few pages earlier they are referred to as "mush."

8. Answers will vary. Some possibilities are that he recognizes the skill and determination it took to catch a marlin as big as the one Santiago caught and he wants to learn more from Santiago. It may be that he recognizes the suffering Santiago endured and believes that he can alleviate it in the future. It also may be that he just doesn't want his friend to be alone anymore.

9. Answers will vary. The final scene—Santiago dreaming once again of the lions—may suggest that Santiago's situation is unchanged. He ends the story still dreaming of lions and preparing once again to venture out to sea. This may be seen as either positive—Santiago has not been ultimately defeated by the events we have just seen unfold—or negative—nothing has changed for Santiago; he still hasn't brought home a fish, and he must venture out again.

10. Answers will vary. Early in the story some of the fishermen made fun of Santiago while others showed him pity. Manolin's parents thought he was bad luck. Now the fishermen seem excited and impressed by the size of Santiago's marlin. They seem to recognize some of the hardship of the last several days.

11. Answers will vary. Because of his injuries, poverty, and failure to bring the fish in whole, it is possible to see Santiago as little more than a skeleton of his former self. On the other hand, he defeated the fish and came back alive and he still has the pride of his skills, the knowledge of his feat, and the respect and friendship of Manolin.

Overview

1. Answers will vary. Students may see the conflict as either man vs. his environment as demonstrated through Santiago's battle with the marlin far out at sea, or man vs. himself as reflected in Santiago's conversations with himself.

2. Answers may vary. How one views the climax of the novel will depend greatly on how one views the main conflict. If the main conflict is considered to be Santiago's battle against nature, then the climax occurs when Santiago kills the marlin or when the sharks destroy the marlin. However, if the main conflict is considered to be Santiago's interior struggle, then we might view the climax occurring just after Santiago returns to his village. At this point, Santiago is at his lowest point. He seems to have been defeated at last, but through Manolin's encouragement, he prepares to go out fishing again.

3. Answers will vary. Again, how one views the resolution of the novel will depend on how one views the main conflict. If the conflict is seen as man vs. nature, then there doesn't seem to be a satisfying resolution. We expect that Santiago will set out to sea again and may face a similar battle with nature. We have only witnessed one battle in this ongoing conflict. However, if one views the conflict as man vs. himself, then we witness Santiago's ability to rally himself. He has not been permanently defeated at the end of the novel and prepares to set out fishing once again.

4. Answers may vary. Hemingway seems to be suggesting that there is something unconquerable in the human spirit. Santiago puts this directly when he says that a man can be destroyed but not defeated. In the novel we see Santiago triumph over the marlin, and then as the sharks take the marlin piece by piece, Santiago refuses to give up the fight. In the end, though Santiago is seemingly defeated, he makes plans to go fishing again. Put more generally, Hemingway may be saying that courage and perseverance can help one survive in the midst of an unfair and difficult world.

5. Answers may vary. Accept reasonable responses. Minor themes may include the unfairness of life (recall Santiago's encounter with the tired warbler and his thoughts about the hawks that the warbler must eventually face) or the importance of friendships (note Santiago's relationship with Manolin).

6. Answers may vary. Students may have very different responses to this question. Some may see Santiago as a static character who ends the story in the same situation we find him in at the beginning. Others may consider him to be a dynamic character who has been changed by his experience at sea. By the end of the story, Santiago's hope seems to be

lost. He speaks of having bad luck—something he'd dismissed earlier. It is only after Manolin speaks of going fishing with him that Santiago seems to be back to his old self. Accept reasonable responses.

7. Hemingway may be attempting to draw a parallel to Christ carrying his own cross along the road to Golgotha.

8. Answers will vary. Santiago does manage to catch the marlin, and he suffers much during the battle. Though he is not able to bring the fish back to the village intact, many of the fishermen from the village take note of the marlin's skeleton and admire and recognize Santiago's accomplishment. It may be said that Santiago is redeemed in the eyes of his fellow fishermen. They may no longer consider him a failure. His suffering also reunites him with Manolin. However, the element of redemption is tenuous, and well-supported opposing views are acceptable. This is also true for whether the Christ-figure analogy is justified.

9. Answers may vary. Santiago is typically viewed as a tragic hero because his desire to "go out too far" to get a big fish results in his downfall. Santiago may be seen as a traditional hero by students who believe that he has triumphed over his loss by the end of the story.

10. Answers will vary. Accept well-reasoned answers. However, to believe that someone is at fault for all things seems to presuppose that people can foresee all consequences to their actions, which is unjustified. For instance, Santiago went out to the deep ocean because he felt he could catch a fish there. He could not foresee the size of the fish, nor that it would drag him so far out to sea. A good example of this is when Santiago berates himself for not splashing seawater against the side of the boat earlier to give himself salt for his fish. In hindsight that is a good idea, but he could not *foresee* that he would need salt later. The verse in Ecclesiastes admits that sometimes our strength and wisdom cannot always prepare, protect, or save us—sometimes circumstances and chance are the controlling factors.

11. Answers will vary. Santiago and Manolin seem to love and respect each other. They have shared many hardships and adventures in their fishing and have an easy acceptance of each other. Manolin recognizes and has faith in the old man's skill and patience, and Santiago accepts the boy's vigor and enthusiasm. The conflict in their relationship comes from the outside—Manolin's parents do not want him to fish with the old man because they fear he is unlucky. This is resolved, in a sense, when Manolin vows to rejoin Santiago again. The verses speak of the difficulty of one person working alone and the strengths and abilities gained by partnership. This is borne out by Santiago's experiences at sea.

12. Answers will vary. The verses from Proverbs seem to presage the "American dream" and the "American work ethic"—anyone can get ahead if he works hard enough. However, sometimes the wicked prosper and the godly fall, or the lucky get rich and the diligent are bankrupt. One explanation is that Proverbs is a collection of God-inspired wise sayings, but not promises or prophetic messages such as are found elsewhere. They represent godly principles, traits, and actions but do not act as a covenant. The passage in Ecclesiastes reflects the writer's observations, not the world as God intended. The world is in a state of sin and rebellion from God and bad things will happen to good and godly people. It may be beneficial to students to search the Gospels for passages in which Jesus warns his disciples of hardships they will face, how they are instructed to act, and how they are reassured.